This igloo book belongs to:

....

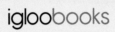

Published in 2015
by Igloo Books Ltd
Cottage Farm
Sywell
NN6 0BJ
www.igloobooks.com

GUA006 1015
2 4 6 8 10 9 7 5 3 1
ISBN 978-1-78557-400-9

Illustrated by Marina Le Ray

Printed and manufactured in China

The Wheels on the Bus

igloobooks

The wheels on the bus go round and round,
round and round, round and round.
The wheels on the bus go round and round, all day long.

The animals in the line go natter, natter, natter,
natter, natter, natter, natter, natter, natter.
The animals in the line go natter, natter, natter, all day long.

The doors on the bus go open and shut,
open and shut, open and shut.
The doors on the bus go open and shut, all day long.

The money on the bus goes clink, clink, clink,
clink, clink, clink, clink, clink, clink.
The money on the bus goes clink, clink, clink, all day long.

The bell on the bus goes ding, ding, ding,
ding, ding, ding, ding, ding, ding.
The bell on the bus goes ding, ding, ding, all day long.

The monkey on the bus goes oo-oo-oo,
oo-oo-oo, oo-oo-oo.
The monkey on the bus goes oo-oo-oo, all day long.

The engine on the bus goes vroom, vroom, vroom,
vroom, vroom, vroom, vroom, vroom, vroom.
The engine on the bus goes vroom, vroom, vroom, all day long.

The horn on the bus goes beep, beep, beep,
beep, beep, beep, beep, beep, beep.
The horn on the bus goes beep, beep, beep, all day long.

The mummies on the bus say, "I love you,
I love you, I love you."
The mummies on the bus say, "I love you," all day long.

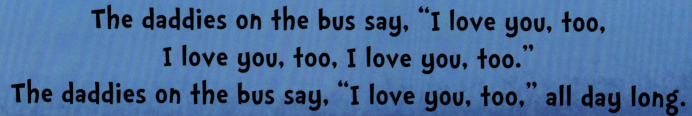

The daddies on the bus say, "I love you, too,
I love you, too, I love you, too."
The daddies on the bus say, "I love you, too," all day long.

The wipers on the bus go swish, swish, swish,
swish, swish, swish, swish, swish, swish.
The wipers on the bus go swish, swish, swish, all day long.

The lights on the bus go flash, flash, flash,
flash, flash, flash, flash, flash, flash.
The lights on the bus go flash, flash, flash, all day long.

The babies on the bus cry, "Wah, wah, wah,
wah, wah, wah, wah, wah, wah."
The babies on the bus cry, "Wah, wah, wah," all day long.

The children on the bus go giggle, giggle, giggle,
giggle, giggle, giggle, giggle, giggle, giggle.
The children on the bus go giggle, giggle, giggle, all day long.

The traffic lights outside go stop, wait, go,
stop, wait, go, stop, wait, go.
The traffic lights outside go stop, wait, go, all day long.

The signals on the bus go blink, blink, blink,
blink, blink, blink, blink, blink, blink.
The signals on the bus go blink, blink, blink, all day long.

The grandpas on the bus go snore, snore, snore,
snore, snore, snore, snore, snore, snore.
The grandpas on the bus go snore, snore, snore, all day long.

The grandmas on the bus go knit, knit, knit,
knit, knit, knit, knit, knit, knit.
The grandmas on the bus go knit, knit, knit, all day long.

The animals on the bus shout, "Here's our stop!
Here's our stop! Here's our stop!"
The animals on the bus shout, "Here's our stop!" all day long.

The wheels on the bus go round and round,
round and round, round and round.
The wheels on the bus go round and round, all day long.

All day long.